BEAUTY AND THE BEAK

HOW SCIENCE, TECHNOLOGY, AND A 3D-PRINTED BEAK RESCUED A BALD EAGLE

By Deborah Lee Rose and Jane Veltkamp

Photos by Glen Hush, Michele Barker,
and the U.S. Fish and Wildlife Service National Digital Library

PERSNICKETY PRESS

Designed by Patricia Mitter

Library of Congress Cataloging-in-Publication
Data available.

ISBN: 978-1-943978-28-1

Manufactured in China

0 9 8 7 6 5 4 3 2 1

*For Ken, who shares the wonder of
watching eagles with me—DLR*

*For Don, who shoulders with me the
challenges and rewards of helping
birds of prey—JV*

Produced by
Persnickety Press
20A North Salem Street
Apex, NC 27502
Persnickety-Press.com

cpsia tracking label information
Production Location: Everbest Printing, Guangdong, China
Production Date: 3/20/2017
Cohort: Batch No. 68113

MIX
Paper from
responsible sources
FSC® C124385

By buying products with the FSC label you
are supporting the growth of responsible
forest management worldwide

BEAUTY
AND THE
BEAK

In a huge nest of twigs, high above an icy cold Alaskan river, a Bald Eagle chick cracked open her egg. For two days, the baby eagle had scraped her beak against the inside of the eggshell. Now she pushed hard with her head till the eggshell split open. She was out!

The cold wind swept over the large eagle nest perched in a tall, old tree. The eaglet was covered only in thin gray and white down. She shivered in the freezing air, until her mother tucked the baby under her own warm body.

Even before the eagle chick could see, she started to take bits of fish from her parents' beaks into her beak.

Soon, her wings became longer and stronger. In one month she could see, stand on her own, and begin to tear food with her own beak. By six weeks, she was almost as big as her parents, with a wingspan of more than six feet.

Bit by bit, her body became covered with the thousands of feathers she would need to fly and keep warm. She used her beak to preen her feathers every day. She cleaned and smoothed them, shifted them to stay warm or cool off, and waterproofed them with oil from a gland near her tail.

By early summer, the young eagle watched while other eagles soared and swooped over the river. One day she was hopping and flapping around the nest, when a sudden gust of wind lifted her into the air. For a moment, she was flying!

All summer, she took longer and longer flights. In time she learned to hunt fish from the river, but when winter came again, the river surface froze. Now the eagle had to search far from home to find food and open water that was not frozen.

She flew thousands of miles,
soaring over mountains and valleys,
cities and farms, always on the lookout for
new sources of food.

Older and stronger eagles sometimes chased or attacked her if
she flew through their territory. The older eagle would lock talons
with her. Then the two birds would spin like a helicopter down
through the sky, until she let go and flew away.

Once the eagle found safer territory with plenty of prey, she became a powerful hunter. From high in the sky, she spotted fish swimming in shallow water.

Then she dove down and sped over the water with her feet thrust out in front of her. She grabbed her prey by locking her sharp talons in place, and carried off the fish she had caught.

By the time she was four years old, the eagle's head and tail feathers started to turn white. Her beak and eyes began to turn golden yellow.

At last, she was ready for the long trip back to the river where she had learned to fly. There she would find a mate. Together they would use their beaks to build and shape a nest of twigs where they could raise their own eaglets.

When the eagle reached the river, she swooped down to catch a silvery salmon from the fast-moving water. The fish was so heavy, she couldn't lift it! She clenched her talons tightly around it and swam to the shore, using her wings like oars to row.

The eagle was so hungry, she ate every bit of fish, ripping off bite after bite of food with her sharp, hooked beak. Then she flew to a thick tree branch to rest and preen her feathers.

Suddenly a crash like lightning and thunder split the air! The eagle's face burned. She couldn't see. Her talons lost their grip and the tree seemed to spin around her. She fell to the ground, stunned. The sun was still high in the sky, but the eagle's world went dark.

A bullet had shattered her beak. Her eye was torn and her face was bleeding. It even hurt for her to breathe. The eagle lay on the ground for days, too weak to move.

As time passed, she recovered enough to walk a short distance, but she could not fly or hunt. Now she had no top beak with which to preen her feathers or tear her food to eat. Her tongue was open to the air and dried out. She could barely scoop up water to drink.

Each day the eagle grew weaker. She was starving.

A policeman found her at a landfill trying to peck for food among the garbage. She wasn't strong enough to fight. He was able to wrap her in a blanket and take her to a wildlife center.

There, the people cleaned and bandaged her wounded face, and gave her medicine to stop any infection.

They named her Beauty.

Beauty's injuries took many months to heal, but her beak didn't grow back. She couldn't eat or drink without human help.

The wildlife center had no room to keep her any longer, and in the wild she would die.

One day a visitor came—a raptor biologist named Janie. Janie's job was to help sick and injured birds of prey like eagles, owls, hawks, falcons, and ospreys. As soon as she saw Beauty, Janie knew she had to find a way to give the eagle a new beak.

Janie took Beauty to her raptor center in Idaho. She and some volunteers built an outdoor aviary as big as a school bus. There, Beauty could live and take short flights.

Janie traveled all around, teaching people about raptors, and sharing Beauty's story. An engineer named Nate came with his daughters to hear Janie speak.

When Janie shared her idea of making a prosthetic beak that would look and move like Beauty's real beak, Nate said, "I think I can help you with Beauty."

N
ate had never worked with animals, but he and Janie both knew that bioengineers made replacement body parts for humans.

First, Janie got her own dentist's assistants, Carol and Cori, to make dental molds that showed the exact shape of Beauty's broken beak. With a laser scanner, Nate took measurements from those dental molds and from a model of a female Bald Eagle's skull. Putting all the measurements together, he used computer code to design the new beak's shape and how it would fit.

Nate printed out the beak on a 3D printer. The printer made the beak from Nate's computer design, building up layer upon layer of melted plastic that hardened into shape. Janie chose the golden yellow color for the prosthetic beak to make Beauty look as she did in the wild.

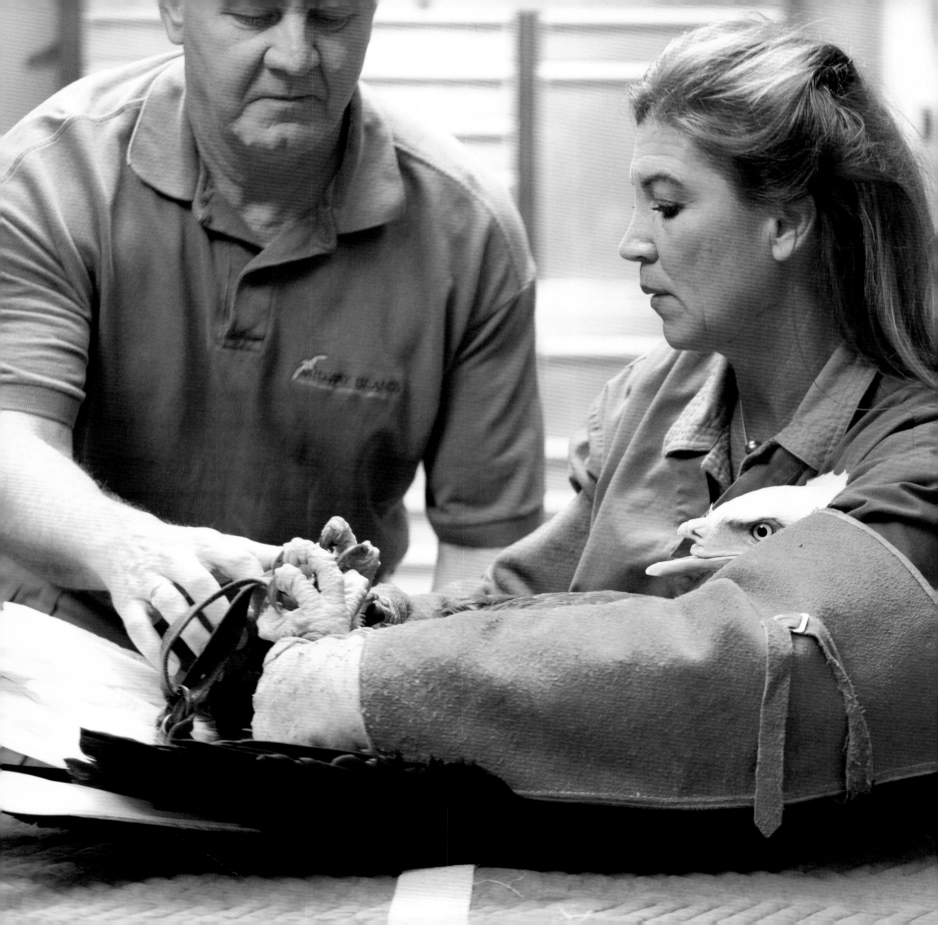

After hundreds of hours of work, and many tests to fit the beak perfectly, the big day came to attach it. Janie wrapped Beauty's wings to keep her from moving. For three hours, Janie never left Beauty's side.

This time, Nate's own dentist, Ryan, had come to help attach the new beak. He and Janie put a small metal rod into Beauty's upper beak. The rod would anchor the new beak in place.

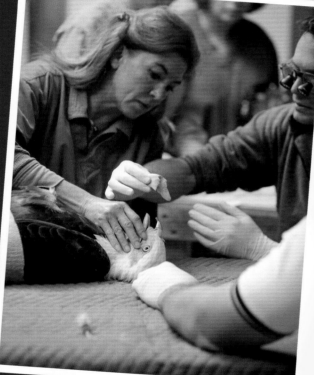

But just when they were ready to glue the beak on, Beauty started to struggle. Her wings were so strong, she burst open the wrap around them. She thrashed her wings, trying to fly away.

"You're all right, big girl. We're here to help you," said Janie. She stroked Beauty's feathers to calm her. Beauty looked straight at Janie and quieted down.

When Beauty was still, they tried the beak on again. Janie could see that Beauty's tongue wasn't moving right. Ryan had to use his dentist's grinding tool to carve out more space on the inside of the beak.

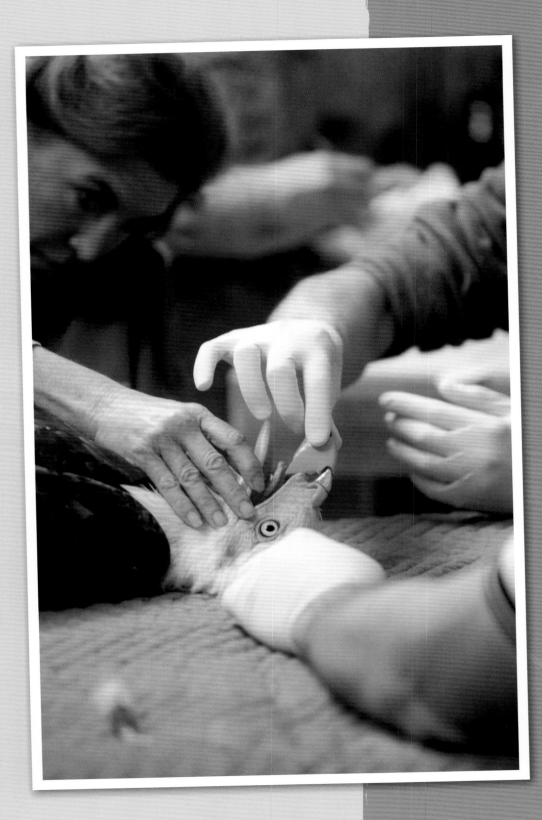

Finally, everything was ready. Ryan spread dental glue on the broken edge of Beauty's top beak. Then he slid the new beak onto the metal rod.

Janie held the beak tightly in place until the glue dried.

When she took her hands away, the 3D-printed beak looked almost as real as Beauty's own beak. But would the new beak work?

Janie knew Beauty was very thirsty after her hours of surgery. Janie unwrapped Beauty's wings and carried her back to the aviary, setting her on her drinking perch.

Beauty didn't hesitate. For the first time since she'd been shot, she leaned down, scooped up a full beak of water, threw back her head and swallowed—just like an eagle in the wild.

Where is Beauty today?

Beauty lives at Birds of Prey Northwest, the raptor facility Janie founded in northern Idaho. Beauty looks out over a large lake from her aviary, which is among the aviaries of many other eagles and raptors in Janie's care.

Beauty can never return to the wild because she cannot survive without care and help from humans. It takes three people together to preen her feathers, trim the feathers around her damaged eye, and clip her talons. Her food—strips of meat and fish—and her water are set out specially every day so she can eat and drink on her own.

Does Beauty still wear the prosthetic beak?

Beauty's real beak has been slowly **regenerating** (growing back) and changing shape, a tiny bit at a time. Now the prosthetic beak no longer fits. Scientists know very little about how a Bald Eagle's beak grows naturally after it has been badly damaged, or if it can grow back completely. Janie has been measuring and photographing Beauty's natural beak as it grows. This new scientific data could help scientists understand more about raptor biology.

Beauty's Beak and Other Prosthetic Devices

Janie was determined that Beauty's new prosthetic beak should look natural and work like her real beak. While the new beak was in place, Beauty was able to use it to eat pre-cut food, to drink, and to **preen** (groom) her feathers. However, the new beak was not as strong as a real eagle beak, and could not bear the tremendous force required for an eagle to rip pieces of food from its prey. The color for the material used in 3D printing the beak was chosen to make the beak look as natural as possible. The prosthetic beak's "Bald Eagle yellow" color is actually a 1970s car color.

New developments in science and engineering are leading to all kinds of prosthetic parts that can bend, flex, absorb force, and work very much like real body parts. Depending on the need and the type of patient, whether human or other kind of animal, engineering a replacement body part may bring together experts from many different fields and careers. Experts may include engineers, doctors and other health professionals, computer programmers, biologists, veterinarians, and scientists who invent new materials. Thanks to 3D printing, families, teachers, students, and human patients themselves are also designing prosthetic body parts.

A person may need a prosthetic limb if she or he was born without that limb, or lost the limb because of disease or an accident. Soldiers and civilians hurt in war may also need prosthetic limbs. Affordable 3D printers are making some prosthetic limbs much less expensive and more available around the world. For example, children who need prosthetic hands can now more easily get new, properly sized hands as their bodies grow. People who live far from hospitals or prosthetics clinics no longer need to wait months or years for replacement limbs.

The Bald Eagle as U.S. Symbol

The Bald Eagle is part of the Great Seal of the United States. The seal became official on June 20, 1782, and in 1789 the Bald Eagle was named the U.S. national bird. Its image is also on the U.S. Presidential Seal, U.S. currency like this quarter, and many other places.

U.S. APOLLO 11

The U.S. Apollo 11 spacecraft carried a lunar landing module called *Eagle*. When the lunar module landed on the moon's surface on July 20, 1969, astronaut Neil Armstrong radioed from the module to NASA Mission Control in Houston, "The *Eagle* has landed." The Apollo 11 mission patch on the astronauts' spacesuits showed a spread-winged Bald Eagle landing on the Moon.

A Note from Raptor Biologist Janie Veltkamp

The Bald Eagle is the national symbol of the United States, but when these eagles are hurt, whose job is it to rescue and care for them and other birds of prey? I believe it's a responsibility we all share!

What humans have learned from the harm done to Bald Eagles in the past, especially from use of the insect spray DDT, is an important reminder for us today. Eagles and other birds of prey are bioindicators or sentinels of the health of the environment. This means that they show the effects of harm to the environment before humans are affected, and tell us how well we are caring for the planet.

Once a threatened and endangered species, Bald Eagles have made a remarkable comeback. Humans—the very species that put Bald Eagles in harm's way—are now working to protect them.

Janie Veltkamp, Birds of Prey Northwest, Idaho

Janie Veltkamp cares for Beauty and other raptors under permit from the U.S. Fish and Wildlife Service.

All About Bald Eagles

Species name *Haliaeetus leucocephalus*

Bald Eagles are one of ten species of sea-eagle or fish-eagle: Bald Eagle, Steller's Sea-Eagle, White-tailed Eagle, Pallas's Fish-Eagle, Sanford's Sea-Eagle, White-bellied Sea-Eagle, African Fish-Eagle, Madagascar Fish-Eagle, Lesser Fish-Eagle, and Gray-headed Fish-Eagle.

Wild Bald Eagles are found only in North America, in all U.S. states except Hawaii. They are also found in Canada and northern Mexico. Bald Eagles nest and migrate along rivers, lakes, reservoirs, other freshwater bodies, and coastal ocean waters. In deepest winter, large numbers fly to places where the water hasn't frozen and there's plenty of food. When food and water become limited, Bald Eagles must share their territory, and will gather in groups of sometimes more than a hundred. Large gatherings of Bald Eagles are called **convocations**.

WINGS AND FEATHERS

Bald Eagles reach adult size at just six to eight weeks old, with a wingspan of 6–7 feet (about 2 meters) wide. A female Alaskan Bald Eagle like Beauty is one of Earth's largest birds. Female Bald Eagles are always larger than males. This helps the females incubate their eggs and defend the nest from predators.

Bald Eagles weigh only about 9–14 pounds (4–6 kilograms). This is because they have hollow bones and air sacs throughout their bodies, as do all birds. Their lighter body, hollow bones, broad wings, and thousands of feathers help them overcome gravity for flight.

Bald Eagles aren't bald. "Balde" means "white" in Old English and refers to the color of adult Bald Eagles' head feathers. The eagles start out with fluffy gray down, which is replaced by mottled dark brown and white feathers. At this young stage, they're often mistaken for Golden Eagles (the only other North American eagle species). By five years of age, an adult Bald Eagle's body feathers are charcoal black, and its head and tail feathers are white.

Adult Bald Eagles have 7,000–8,000 feathers. They keep warm or cool off by shifting their feathers to let more or less air between the feather layers. A Bald Eagle preens, or grooms, its feathers with its beak. It does so by splitting open hard quills (narrow tubes) that hold new feathers, opening up the feathers, smoothing the feathers into interlocking layers, and spreading oil, from a gland near its tail, throughout its feathers to waterproof them.

Bald Eagles have seven more bones in their neck than humans. This makes the eagle's neck extra flexible, so the eagle can reach all its feathers with its beak. When the eagle sleeps, it turns its head toward the back of its body and covers its head with its feathers to keep it warm. This can make a sleeping Bald Eagle look like it has no head!

Bald Eagles shed or molt their feathers every year, over several months. As old feathers are shed, new feathers replace them. Native Americans highly prize eagle feathers which are very important to their tribal cultures. Native Americans are the only people in the U.S. who are legally allowed to have eagle feathers. Naturally molted feathers collected from eagles are used in the making of fans, headdresses, and other accessories for tribal ceremonies. Janie Veltamp works with the Coeur d'Alene Tribe in the Pacific Northwest, training tribal members to house and care for eagles that cannot be returned to the wild, so that their molted feathers can be used by the Tribe.

BEAK

A Bald Eagle uses its hooked beak to rip off pieces of its prey to eat, scoop up water to drink, preen its feathers, arrange sticks to build its nest, and feed and protect its young. Even before it hatches, a baby Bald Eagle uses a sharp tooth on its tiny beak to crack open the eggshell from inside. The tooth disappears a few weeks later.

The Bald Eagle's beak is made of keratin, as are other bird beaks and human fingernails. An eagle sheds and replaces its beak's outer layers throughout its life. After eating, a Bald Eagle rubs its beak against the tree branch or rock where it's feeding. This behavior, called **feaking**, keeps the beak in perfect shape.

NEST

Bald Eagles mate for life, and may return to the same **aerie** (nest) year after year. Some nests have been used for more than a hundred years, by many generations of one Bald Eagle family. A Bald Eagle nest is the largest nest of any North American bird. An old nest can weigh over 1,000 pounds (450 kilograms).

Bald Eagles build their tornado-shaped nests in tall trees, where a thick branch meets the tree trunk to create a "Y." An eagle carries twigs to the nest using its feet, and weaves the twigs in an interlocking pattern using its beak. Eagles may add sticks until the nest is an average 6–8 feet (2–2.4 meters) wide. They line the nest with moss, leaves, and other soft materials.

An eagle family uses the nest for three months. The female lays her eggs and both parents sit on the eggs to incubate them. Bald Eagle parents feed and take care of their young in the nest until the eaglets fly off to hunt on their own. The parents may leave the nest to migrate, or stay nearby until the next breeding season.

FLIGHT

When eagles are about 10–12 weeks old, they **fledge** (take their first short flights), returning to the nest after each flight. If a young eagle can't get back to the nest and lands on another branch or the ground, it lets out a special food-begging cry. This alerts the parents to bring food to wherever the eaglet is. Parents feed the young eagle there until it's ready to try again to fly back to the nest.

Adult Bald Eagles fly so high that even pilots of commercial airplanes have seen the eagles in their flight path. Bald Eagles can soar for hours, barely flapping their broad, planklike wings as they ride on rising currents of warm air called **thermals**. These are created when sunlight heats the ground, the warm ground heats the air, and the warm air rises.

Depending on their prey, Bald Eagles use different flight patterns for hunting. A Bald Eagle can streak down through the sky at 100 miles (160 km) per hour or the eagle can fly low and slow over water, feet thrust out in front, to snatch up fish right out of the water.

FEET

Bald Eagles grab live prey with sharp talons on their feet. They clamp their talons around the prey by tightening muscles and tendons in their feet and lower legs. Once the tendons tighten, they **ratchet** (lock in place) bit by bit. This keeps the talons clenched as long as the eagle needs to hold on to its prey or a perching branch.

Bald Eagle feet have another adaptation for hunting—sticky, bumpy pads called **spicules** on the bottoms. Spicules help an eagle hold onto a slippery fish while the talons are locking into place. As the pads wear away, new ones grow in to replace them.

EYES

All raptors, including owls, hawks, falcons, ospreys and especially eagles, are known for their keen eyesight. A Bald Eagle's eyeballs are much smaller than a human's, but a Bald Eagle has eight times the power to see details over long distances. From high in the air, Bald Eagles can spot fish swimming in shallow water.

Bald Eagles can see forward and to the side at the same time. Though its eyeballs don't move, the eagle can rotate its head to see a wide visual range. Eagles see in color, unlike owls which are nocturnal and see only in black and white. A Bald Eagle's color vision helps it find prey even when the prey is camouflaged.

Endangered No Longer

Half a million Bald Eagles once lived in North America, but by the 1970s, they were headed toward extinction in the U.S. lower 48 states. They had been hunted by humans for hundreds of years, and been harmed by use of an insecticide called DDT, which was widely used to kill mosquitoes and insects that fed on crops and gardens. Before DDT was finally banned from use in the U.S. in 1972, it had contaminated streams, rivers, lakes, and other bodies of water, as well as the organisms living there.

When eagles ate contaminated fish and other animals, they produced eggshells so thin that the shells broke before the eaglets inside could hatch. The DDT caused a reduction in the amount of calcium contained in the shells. The same eggshell-thinning problem affected ospreys and peregrine falcons.

In her famous book *Silent Spring*, environmentalist Rachel Carson wrote that DDT was so dangerous to the eagle population, it might "make it necessary for us to find a new national emblem." By 1967, Bald Eagles were a protected species. Forty years later, in 2007, they were taken off the Endangered and Threatened Species list. Their recovery was helped by protection from the Endangered Species Act and the end of DDT use in the U.S.

To conserve Bald Eagles, their populations had to be protected and rebuilt. Biologists launched a nationwide effort to help bring back Bald Eagles in places where they had nearly or completely disappeared. The biologists relocated hundreds of eaglets from places where Bald Eagles were not endangered—like Alaska, Wisconsin, Minnesota, and parts of Canada—to the many U.S. states where the number of eagles was critically low.

The biologists moved the eaglets when they were about 4-6 weeks old, before the birds had learned to fly. In their new regions, the eaglets were kept in protected, artificial nests on special towers. Biologists took on the role of eagle "parents"—though staying out of sight—to make sure the eaglets had food and water and were safe from any predators. The eaglets imprinted on their new habitats and took their first flights there. When they became adults, they nested and raised their families **not** where they themselves had hatched, but where they had learned to fly.

Eagles Still at Risk

Bald Eagles keep their ecosystem in balance by hunting other live animals. Bald Eagles are top predators, but if a young eagle can't learn to hunt, it will die. Some 70% of young Bald Eagles don't survive their first year. Even if they do survive, they still face many dangers.

Bald Eagles are protected by the U.S. Fish and Wildlife Service, but their natural behaviors put them at risk from human activity and technology. Soaring and perching eagles are easy targets for poachers. Shooting an eagle is against U.S. law, but illegal shooting is a leading cause of Bald Eagle deaths.

Bald Eagles can get hurt or killed when they collide with power lines, cars, or trains. Bald Eagles are also scavengers. Eagles that feed on dead animals by the roadside may collide with moving cars while trying to fly out of the way.

If an eagle (or other raptor) feeds on an animal that was shot with a lead bullet, the eagle ends up digesting tiny bits of lead along with the meat. Over time, the digested lead particles poison the eagle and harm its nervous system. This makes the bird lose its balance and ability to fly. Lead poisoning can kill an eagle slowly over a period of weeks. Eagles also get poisoned if they eat rodents killed with rodent poison, or poisoned meat used as bait to kill other wildlife such as wolves and coyotes.

When Bald Eagles Need Care

If you find a wounded, sick, or stranded Bald Eagle or other raptor, contact a raptor rehabilitation center, wildlife center, or state wildlife agency. The sooner a raptor gets proper care, the greater its chance of surviving. Raptor rehabilitation centers like Birds of Prey Northwest, as well as some wildlife centers, rescue and give medical treatment to hurt and sick Bald Eagles. Some eagles recover and can go back into the wild. Eagles that can't be released may live at a center because they're too disabled to fly and hunt, and need special care.

How You Can Help

- You may be able to volunteer to help at a raptor or wildlife center, or you can become a member to support the center.

- You can ask your teacher or parent to invite a raptor educator to speak at your school or community event. Have the educator bring a live Bald Eagle or other raptor if possible.

- Your words and actions can help keep Bald Eagles and other raptors safe from loss of wild habitat, illegal poaching, poisoning, and environmental hazards. Support efforts to protect eagles and raptors by posting on social media and sending letters, emails, and tweets to community and government leaders, public agencies, wildlife organizations, and news media.

Resources

Birds of Prey Northwest
Northern Idaho
Janie Veltkamp, Founding Director
BirdsOfPreyNorthwest.org
The nonprofit raptor education and
rehabilitation center where Beauty lives
and where thousands of raptors have been
given medical treatment with the purpose of
returning them to the wild

- Educational guide to *Beauty and the Beak*
- Instructions for obtaining 3D printing STL
  file (© Jane Veltkamp) to make a lifesize
  replica of Beauty's prosthetic beak on a 3D
  printer
- Contact information about Beauty, author
  visits, and live raptor programs
- Video about Beauty

Engineering is Elementary Curriculum
Museum of Science, Boston
eie.org/engineering-everywhere/curriculum-
units/prosthetics
Hands-on STEM activities to make and
test simple models of Beauty's prosthetic
beak, in Engineering Everywhere/"Go Fish:
Engineering Prosthetic Tails" educator guide
and student notebook

The Cornell Lab of Ornithology
Cornell University
AllAboutBirds.org/guide/Bald_Eagle/id

The Raptor Center
University of Minnesota
raptor.umn.edu

U.S. Fish and Wildlife Service Migratory Bird
Program
fws.gov/migratorybirds/baldeagle.htm

U.S. Fish and Wildlife Service National Digital
Library
digitalmedia.fws.gov/cdm/landingpage/
collection/natdiglib

U.S. National Park Service
nps.gov/yell/learn/nature/baldeagle.htm

U.S. National Wildlife Refuge System
fws.gov/refuges/whm/viewBaldEagles.html

National Wildlife Federation
nwf.org/wildlife/wildlife-library/birds/bald-
eagle.aspx

Audubon
Audubon.org/field-guide/bird/bald-eagle

The **Cornell** Lab of Ornithology

What You Can Do to Learn More

LISTEN TO THE SOUNDS OF A BALD EAGLE

What does a Bald Eagle sound like? You might be surprised. Listen now by scanning this symbol with the Bird QR app or visit the Cornell Lab of Ornithology's All About Birds website to hear additional sounds, see photos, and learn more at *bit.ly/baldeaglesounds*.

WATCH AN EAGLE CAM

See eagles at their nests up close by watching a live streaming cam. Do an internet search for "eagle cam" during the breeding season (timing will vary depending upon where the nest is located). You might see an eagle hatching or being fed by its parents!

DOWNLOAD A BALD EAGLE PAGE TO COLOR

Color in your very own scene of a Bald Eagle flying in the wild. Download your free coloring page from the Cornell Lab of Ornithology at *bit.ly/baldeaglecoloring*.

FIND OUT WHERE YOU CAN SEE A BALD EAGLE

Are you hoping to see a Bald Eagle in the wild? Visit eBird by scanning this symbol with the Bird QR app or visit *eBird.org*, then choose "Explore Data" to find out where and when bird watchers have seen Bald Eagles near you!

LEARN ABOUT OTHER EAGLES AND RAPTORS

Now that you know all about Bald Eagles, keep your eyes open for other birds of prey, too. You might see a Red-tailed Hawk perched by a roadside, an Osprey nesting on a light pole, or a Peregrine Falcon on a building ledge. Learn about 20 species of raptors by scanning this symbol with the Bird QR app or visit *bit.ly/allaboutraptors*.

HELP BIRDS IN YOUR NEIGHBORHOOD

Set up a bird feeder, plant flowers, or put up a nest box. Use the Bird QR app to scan the symbols below for each topic from the Cornell Lab of Ornithology or type the URLs for each topic into your browser to learn more.

CHOOSE FOOD AND FEEDERS
bit.ly/foodandfeeders

CREATE HABITAT WITH PLANTS
bit.ly/whichbirdswhichplants

BUILD A NEST BOX
bit.ly/rightbirdrighthouse

BIRD QR is a free book companion app created especially for books from the Cornell Lab Publishing Group.

Visit the Apple or Android store to search "Bird QR" and download the app for free. Once downloaded, open the app and touch "Tap To Start" which will bring you to the main menu screen. From there, you can start scanning symbols in the book by touching the "Scan Book QR Now" button or navigate to another page.

Photo Credits

Acknowledgments

Enormous thanks to Pat Redig, DVM, PhD, Lori Arent, and the staff at The Raptor Center of the University of Minnesota, who fundamentally shaped my professional work by training me in the medical standards of raptor care and treatment—JV

Great thanks to Devin Dombrowski of Wildlife Rehabilitation MD who introduced me to my first wild eagle—DLR

Special thanks to the U.S. Fish and Wildlife Service Migratory Bird Permitting Authority and USFWS National Digital Library; in Idaho: to all Birds of Prey Northwest volunteers; Nate Calvin, AeroLEDs; Ryan K. Doyle, DDS and staff, Capitol Dental Center for Implant & Cosmetic Dentistry; Kevin Rogers, DVM and staff, Kootenai Animal Hospital; Todd Schini, DDS, Carol Johnson and Cori Wilson, Schini Family Dentistry; Wayne Melquist; Erica Compton and Angela Hemingway, Idaho STEM Action Center; in Alaska: to staff and volunteers, Bird Treatment and Learning Center; Alaska State Troopers; in South Dakota: to Kristen Veltkamp; in Washington, DC: to Miranda Bogen; in California: to California Teachers Association; Devin Dombrowski and Rachel Avilla, Wildlife Rehabilitation MD; Catherine Halversen, Lawrence Hall of Science; Nick Kloski, HoneyPoint3D; Mia Cichetti; in Colorado, to Libby Mojica, Raptor Research Foundation.

About the Authors

DEBORAH LEE ROSE is an internationally published, award-winning author of many beloved children's books. Her newest book *Beauty and the Beak: How Science, Technology, and a 3D-Printed Beak Rescued a Bald Eagle* is a CALIFORNIA READS recommended title of the California Teachers Association. *Jimmy the Joey: The True Story of an Amazing Koala Rescue* is a Reading is Fundamental/Macy's Multicultural Collection title and Notable Social Studies Trade Book for Students K-12. *Into the A, B, Sea* was named to the New York Public Library *100 Titles for Reading and Sharing*. Deborah helped create and directed communications for the ALA/AASL award-winning, national STEM education website *Howtosmile.org*, and helped create STEM activity apps for Lawrence Hall of Science which have been downloaded more than one million times. She also served as Director of Communications for Lindsay Wildlife Experience, which includes the first wildlife rehabilitation hospital established in the U.S. She lives in Walnut Creek, CA, in the San Francisco Bay area and speaks at book events, conferences, schools, and libraries across the country. Visit her website at *DeborahLeeRose.com*.

JANE VELTKAMP is a raptor biologist and rehabilitator, wildlife educator, trained nurse, and master falconer. She is coauthor of the new book *Beauty and the Beak: How Science, Technology, and a 3D-Printed Beak Rescued a Bald Eagle*, a CALIFORNIA READS recommended title of the California Teachers Association. She led the team who developed Beauty the Bald Eagle's prosthetic beak, and has lifetime care of Beauty. She is founder and executive director of Birds of Prey Northwest, in Idaho, a raptor center which educates the public about raptor conservation, including through live raptor programs, and has provided medical treatment and rehabilitation to thousands of injured birds of prey to return them to the wild. She spent ten years of her career reintroducing Ospreys and Peregrine Falcons to regions where they had disappeared from their habitat in South Dakota and Indiana. She rescues and cares for Bald Eagles, including Beauty, by permit from the U.S. Fish and Wildlife Service. She lives near Coeur d'Alene, Idaho, and is also the eagle expert for the Coeur d'Alene Tribe's Native American Aviaries. Visit her website at *BirdsOfPreyNorthwest.org*.